Gloomy Presentiments Of Things To Come

By
Susurrus Din

B

Dedicated to
Francisco
De Goya and
Hieronymus
Bosch,

Two of many
whom these
authors owe much.

What Lies Herein

With This Ring, I Do Thee Wed
(For Ogdred Weary)

With this ring, I do thee wed.
O, how I shall rejoice when thou art
dead,
Why I may even caper, gambol, or
dance,
Now, how do like your tea,
With arsenic, two lumps, and cream?
Why not go out for a stroll, go on go,
I'll meet you presently beneath the
wheels of my auto.

With my body, I do thee worship,
If not a stumble, why not a slip,
Down the winding stairs,
Why, I haven't care if you are interred
alive,
In a mausoleum, sepulcher, or crypt
besides!

While it be not my intention to
engender suspicion,
Might I at least explain my
odd manner and diction?
I may account for that dagger in my
armoire drawer on Tuesday last,
As for the pistol in the marmalade,
there has been a rash of
Rabid, wily shrews,
Infesting the surrounding glade and
mews!

That West Indies adder on the pantry
floor is an escaped zoological
specimen from Kuala Lumpur!

And with all my worldly goods I thee
endow,
Yet to flee under the cover of night,
My beloved, bride to be, this I shan't
allow!!
Darling, dearest treasure true,
Must we begin our courtship anew?

What of the chocolates, flowers, walks
and choice wines?
Or should I infer as you run,

Raving down the lane,
That you most respectfully-
Decline.

To My Decay, Come What May

My friends,
Pray listen,
As I relate to thee, of how I was prey to
a most grim tragedy.

For I am certain it can be found,
Not in mustiest parchment or,
Arcane book,
The case of another who saw
graveworms wheresoever they looked.

Pardon my darting eyes as my tale I do
tell,
For I fear a worm at any instant may
writhe forth from your chest as well!

It all began on Tuesday last,
I can now admit,
Whence I saw a graveworm 'pon the
gilded frame of my De Goya print,
Soon after at the club,
Were another few,
Inching along the headline whilst,
I read the news.

In the branches of the parks stately,
Trees, swayed most menacingly,
Graveworm leaves,
The confectionary shop on the next
street was fully stocked with
Graveworm sweets,
Every bric-a-brac shop and such like
place were overrun with these blasted
graveworms of late!

The apothecary where I made my
bread,
Gave me no relief from my dread,
As every philter and tincture that I
sought to take,
Was filled with graveworms,
Graveworms of every shape!

When my for my wife's aid I did plead
and entreat,
She merely laughed a deluge of grave
worms at her dainty feet.

My repast gave me no quarter,
As my meal consisted of more of the
squirming monsters,
When brought from the larder

Nor from my fellow man could I find relief,
When a passerby from whom I solicited the time,
Drew a teeming mass of the devils from his great coat-
Grotesquely beslimed!

To meet with another graveworm or plunge into river Thames?
Grant me no life said I than a life with them!
And with a leap,
Mad as a hatter,
I most decidedly choose the latter.

Stay your shrieks and yells,
The most horrid is yet to tell,
For as I sank into those darkly depths this much can be said,
So died a single graveworm bound in a pouch of my hair and nails under my bed.

Pretty Poison

Oh be swift,
Oh be stealthy,
My poison,
My poison deadly.

Added drop by drop,
To your daily cup of chamomile,
And so I feel-
Entirely at ease,

For nothing more remains,
No, not a thing,
Not a thing,
simply to devise some manner of clever
fiction for each of your untimely,
er .....afflictions.

Twas not a simple task,
Not in the least,
Though no matter the grim
circumstance,
I was with a most cunning explanation
replete.
Now then,
If you'd be so kind,

As to allow me to narrate how over the
coming hours,
Thy health takes a most terrible turn
for the dread and dour.

At one past the hour,
You will mildly perspire,
An unseasonable summer is too blame,
Should any inquire.

At hour two,
Thy insides will become a sticky goo,
To which I shall reply, mere indigestion
from spoiled food.

At hour three,
Rant most liberally you will,
Though all know, you always to be
outspoken,
Endlessly talking vile swill.

At hour four,
You will begin to draw up your final
will and testament,
Can you really blame a chap for
wanting his affairs in order?
We should all be as diligent.

At hour five,
The poison has crept into your brain.
By a stay in the madhouse I wilt
suggest to all,
Will he come to his senses again.

At hour six.
The seat of your soul,
Shall in your chest to a stand still,
Alas my brothers and sisters,
I will bemoan,
(Most convincingly I might add),
How can we hope to set ourselves
against our makers will?

What fiendish fun!

Though sadly I cannot stay,
As by the fifth hour, I took my leave,
Having long since fled far away.

To where I sit now aside the fire,
With my cigar and a glass of port,
Ruminating on how,
What I did once for revenge,
I mean to do again for sport.

On The Seventh Day Of Torture, My Torturer Gave To Me...

On Monday, it was the stocks,
Head,
Arms,
lock-lock.

On Tuesday, the rack,
Crick,
Crick,
Crack-crack.

On Wednesday, I was dunked,
alas,
if I'd only sunk.

On Thursday, the wheel and flail,
Lash,
Lash,
Wail-wail.

On Friday, buried to the neck,
Nibble,
Nibble,
Peck-peck.

On Saturday, twas the Judas Chair,
Pull,
Pull,
tear-tear.

On Sunday, I confess, I confess,
To despoiling crops,
Striking women barren,
And assuming the shape of a wolf,
By diabolical agency, no less.

My Dearest Be Not Dead!

Preposterous!
My dearest be not dead!
My good fellow,
surely thou art disturbed in the head.

My dearest be not dead!
She so enjoys your witty banter,
Why just look at that rictus grin,
Go on, take a gander.

My dearest be not dead!
Be forewarned,
At a game or charades she is most
adept,
Pantomiming, a lifeless corpse for
instance,
Or any such inert object.

My dearest be not dead!
Rigor mortis you say!
By Jove!
Have you not heard that the deathly
pallor look is most en vogue?

Why countless ladies strive in vain to
their great vexation,
For what comes naturally to my
dearest,
That in articulo mortis complexion.

My dearest be not dead!
Granted, she has been sitting
motionless for several hours in your
midst,
I say,
Know thee not of defensive whist?

My dearest be not dead!
How is it every time a moldering finger,
is found on the sandwich tray,
Or some such indiscretion,
Everyone seems to look in our
direction?

My dearest be not dead!
My dearest be not dead!
How many more times need this be
said!

Beg your pardon,
Her head was last seen rolling down,
the hall and into the garden?
I ought to collect it,
I suppose I'd better,
Now that you mention it,
Perhaps she has been a touch under
the weather.

Barnabas Stanislaw Samsa Phrit, THE TRANSFORMED IT!!!! For Franz Kakfa and David Cronenberg

Barnabas Stanislaw Samsa Phrit,
Was an avid collector of avocado pits,
Of every conceivable variety,
Contributing often to the journals of
the scholarly.

Never you mind his many whims and
eccentricities,
Let us speak rather of the curious
metamorphoses,
That changed this most unremarkable
twit,
Into the hideous,
Reviled-- Transformed It!

You are still here?
You have not fled?
Why I was certain to find you cowering
under the bed.

Very well, take head and steel your
nerves,
Against this tale of the strange and
perverse!

Awaking one morn as was his wont,
Barnabas found he was feeling faint
and somewhat gaunt,
At the sight of a mass of squirming
tentacles reaching down to the floor,
Were his ribs had been,
But the evening before.

Tentacles, tentacles, Alas and woe,
What a horror to behold!

Tentacles, tentacles,
By Jove and Egad!

Barnabas cinched his dressing gown
close thinking himself quite mad.
To the looking glass he sped, only to
behold,
A mass of beady, blinking eyes upon
his brow of old,
Oh, how he did shriek and cower in
fright,

For never again would his hat sit quite right.

What could be the cause of this!
Demanded our Dear Barnabas!

Moving to kick the ottoman, an act he was not to complete,
With an amorphous blob, instead of feet.

He would have composed himself by reading the post,
Were it not for the pincer like talons,
Shredding the paper to miniscule motes.

Worst of all, thought Barnabas
Stanislaw Samsa Phrit,
How am I ever to sort another Zutano from a Pinkerton pit!

Pacing his bedchamber Barnabas felt none the better,
When he suddenly took to the air on wings of leather.

Despite the protests of his prized
Siamese cat Aloysius,
Barnabas greedily drained the poor
beast of his vital fluids.

With that he dissevered himself forever
from the world of men,
As such conduct would simply not do
among the esteemed ranks of,
The International Avocado
Commission.

At long last, lowly Barnabas Stanislaw
Samsa Phrit,
Had become the Transformed It!

Abomination they'd cry!

Monstrosity they'd bellow!
He was always such a peculiar fellow!

Even aberrations of natural law,
Have their part to play after all.

Abomination, monstrosity, so be it!

Or so reasoned the former Barnabas
Stanislaw Samsa Phrit.

So oozing from his apartments with
something of a grimace,
To prey on a woefully unwitting
populace.

Horrible Hypnotists Hullabaloo

He's heard, she's heard, they've heard, what of you?

About the Horrible,
Hypnotists,
Hullabaloo.

Oh, it's a ghastly business from beginning to end.
You see there was scarcely a Parisian salon,
Where about Balthazar Von Charlatan they don't prattle on.

Why that Master of Mesmerism,
As he was so coined with great pomp and flair,
Once willed the King of Hungary for an hour quarter,
To sit like a vulture upon a high backed chair.

Across Atlantic waters,
Lies the fair city of New York proper,

Where there arose a commotion most
unseemly,
Around the dinning tables of all those
of noble birth,
And good breeding.

Balderdash!
By what means, and how!
Could one man drive the bankers of the
entire stock exchange,
To wallowing on the floor like common
sows!

Who you may ask is liable?
Why Mortimer Mountebank,
The Hierophant of Hypnosis,
For whom such an act is but a trifle!

As one might guess, two such
personages,
Were most ill disposed to share the
press.

There would to themselves mumble and
mutter,
Why "his" exploits should be
displayed,
Next to the evening's cabarets, that cad,
Whilst I languish there aside this girdle
ad!

Enough!
Said the former,
Quite so!
The latter,
A hypnotist duel will quite settle the
matter.

For far from there lies a deep forest,
In the center of the forest there is a
mountain,
At the mountains peak,
A cave-
This was were destiny appointed their
fates they would did brave.

That and the unseasonable autumn
pleasantness,
Not to mention low levels of counter-
acting,

Electro-aetheric resonance,

By the great cunning of their powers
subliminal,
Would they compel one another to
bethink themselves members of,
Kingdoms,
Animal,
Vegetable,
And Mineral.

They were so evenly matched that one
could not the other dispatch,
Then it happened.

Though how remains a mystery,
'Twas around the time when Balthazar
thought himself an aardvark,
And Mortimer, celery.

Both became fixed,
fixed to the spot.
Not unlike a victrola whose record gets
stuck in one place,
So to could the hypnotists at one
another only-

Gaze,
Gaze,
Gaze.

Neither stirred nor made a sound,
As days followed days and week
followed week,
Why you just had to think,
They would not be in this predicament
if only they blink!

Their clothes all a' tattered,
The hair long and matted,
It was not long before their flesh simply
withered away,
Having no more eyeballs with which
with to gaze.
As best I know they remain there still,
Way atop Dead Hypnotists Hill.

From here dear listener, our tale can
proceed no farther,
As beyond this, we are all left to
wonder.

So spoke the elderly gentlemen to the
dear child at the window,

Pay mind to Mortimer and Balthazar, don't you know,
Or face their gruesome end, you just might,
And remember always,
Why staring at others is most decidedly impolite.

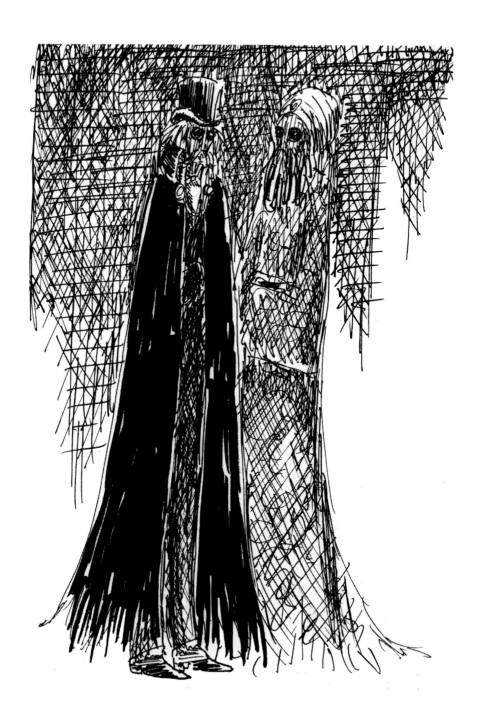

Gilbert the Ghoul

Gilbert the Ghoul was not the most
well-liked in his school.

He was not a ghoul in the sense of a
child with tastes dark and morbid,
More of the kind fond of their food
prepared post-mortem.

The children's aversion had nothing to
do with Gilbert's bulging eyes, fetid
odor or toothy maul.
It was only that his arrival at
Morningside Elementary,
Was too like the overspreading of
some funereal pall.

When a class pet went missing or its
grave desecrated,
Young Gilbert could always be
implicated.

When Bela the gold fish was found
belly up,
Gilbert alone had fishy scales,
Beneath his grimy finger nails.

It was assumed that Claude the parrot
had escaped and flown South,
Until Gilbert was found with a
vermillion feather,
In the corner of his mouth,

The trail of Boris the hamster grisly remains,
Ended at Gilbert's locker,
Yes, the very same.

It soon became evident, beyond a shadow of a doubt,
More school pets were meeting their ends while Gilbert was about.

Could not Gilbert be transferred to another school?
Surely that would rid us once and for all of this Gilbert the Ghoul!

No, there was only recourse left to the merciless tots,
It was decided, for they really were a bloodthirsty lot,

The youngsters massed into an unruly mob just after luncheon,
Outfitting themselves with pitchforks, torches, and stout wooden truncheons.

The children fell upon Gilbert,
Tearing him to ribbons,
And doing him in,
Then buried him in the sandbox,
Right next to the jungle gym.

Obscurum Per Obscurius

For many a month hadst I been
exhuming fresh cadavers at the good
doctor's behest,
For what he so queerly termed, his
empirical "tests"

Though in all my employ as his
resurrectionist,
Never did it occur,
That I collected such a specimen,
So very, shall we say-singular.

In spite of being less than a fortnight
immured,
This corse was black as sable,
And withered so,
As if 'twere a thousand, thousand
years interred.

Possessing none of those tell tale
charnel aromas,
Suffusing the room with rather,
Faint notes of mercury, salt, and
sulphur.

Without delay I dispatched the paige across the moors,
To fetch the doctor here posthaste, he willingly suffered.

Would that I not dismissed my sole company,
For upon my return to that room wherein the body lied,
Such a turn did I have by what I next espied...

That very same corse which was only a moment prior,
As I mentioned,
So strangely blackened,
Wert now stark white,
Eerily iridescent.

Nearer yet I brought the taper,
To ensure confounded senses hath not erred,
Lo, white it was,
Upon my soul, as alabaster fair.

A jot of bitters would steady my nerves, I so reasoned,

Quitting the room for but an instant
nary,
To mine mantle for mine flask I
withdrew,
Without tarry.

Whereupon the hovels center I gained,
Astonied I was to behold,
That body, that body hadst yet again
changed.

Now nearly sanguine in hue,
Though all this time that corse lay
stone still-
It didst not move.

Now, it is just such rural environs,
Where customs do say,
That the murderer appearance causeth,
Blood to ooze forth from the bones of
the slain,
If there be sooth to these tellings,
Which I give no credence,
It would scarcely account,
For the whole form incarnadined thus,
As it be witnessed.

Nay there are other agencies at work!
Agencies that would consign me by
designs to the furthest reaches of
insanity,
Lo, what was once a balmy breeze of
curiosity,
Piquing fancies I canst only intimate,
Art now a maelstrom of the malignity,
Blasting me off the precipice to a most
ruinous fate!

My dagger flew to the ready,
To meet mine destiny by blade point!

I vacillating verily-
Betwixt composed disbelief and a feral
mien
Took leave of my senses, and over to
reverie gave in.

Imagine, a cultivated man of the age,
Stricken with moral vagaries as those
of that cloistered ilk.
Dagger in hand,
All in a rage.

Yet, as I circled round that hovel with
its weird tenant,
An otherworldly sensation pricked my
flesh as it had at no other occasion.

From which nether regions, foul airs,
Or chthonian pit was this cores
expelled?

By whom, by what
Be it endowed?

To what end doth it haunt the earth
anew,
Avenger upon some venial misdeed
begotten,
Long ago committed,
Though not forgotten.

I threw my hands heavenwards
imploring exoneration by the celestial
machinery,
For these mortal remains,
To forebear, O, forebear its ill-starred
charge to claim.

Ere I couldst give utterance to this, a
hand like adamantine
Seized my arm,
Arresting the feeble paroxysm of
protest on my lips.

Held fast in that death pale hand all
became,
Golden beyond golden,
As my life force withered and waned,
Beyond golden,
Beyond golden,
Beyond golden, brightly burnished,

I am no more, no more,
A psychopomp to the purpose.

What felicity I were home when the
Paige paid call,
The door ajar I entered withal.

A gnarled corpse sprawled on the floor
I beheld in a ghastly blackened state,
I can only assume,
This be the one my grave robber made
mention,
And the paige didst relate.

What eludes my reason still to this
very day,
Is why the body was so neatly arrayed,
Bring one finger of the left hand?

Pointing in the moor ward direction,
In the semblance of a final injunction.

Twas to the moors avaunt, I first gazed
on that preternatural glow,
As I recount-

A radiant golden light bore on the
ether overspreading the moors
recesses,
Keeping vigil aside the night and
darkness.

When gazing upon this strange sight,
These words did into my brain alight,
Nay not like a thought,
Were these words wrought,

They were psychically summoned,
From some primeval fount,

For weeks afterward I was told, I could
do naught but repeat,
Interspersed amongst feverish rantings
and wails-
Nature unaided shall fail,
Nature unaided shall fail,
Nature unaided shall fail.

A Hunger Forbade

"What's one mans poison
Is another's meat and drink"

Dark as a murder of crows on a
winter midnight,
Be this dungeon where I lay in my
bonds,
With his remains,
By solitary taper light.

Tell me what recourse I am given,
Afore the rot sets in,
And the devil take him?

If his house of flesh be soon corrupted,
 Then he is not long for the grave,
Not long have I occasion,
Lest I prolong my pangs.

His person I loathe utterly,
With every fiber which I art composed,
All manner of his speech, act, and deed
that issue forth,

Makes for torment,
Whence I suffer his society.

O, for years upon years I can scarce
recollect!
I longed to quit that vile company,
For some lone corner of this dismal
chamber,
Were it not for the chain holding me
fast by the neck!

To load my confinement with misery
upon misery,
The wretch,
He spared no pains,
Even slumber gave no reprieve.

As once I wit in my feigned repose,
Him holding privy counsel with our
keepers,
Who upon their weekly visitation,
Never failed to serve that villain a
larger share,
Of our coarse and meager fare.

Leaving me to mine privations and so,
Twas on this head my rancor took root,
All the rest simply variegated the fruit.

It is well,
He is dead and rotting,

I wilt be undone,
Chained and starving.

Nay it be not well,
Nay it be not well,
Unless I bend my course to Hell?

I fear,
I fear,
The mere courting these unwholesome
thoughts causeth to pass,
The very doom that wilt my soul
ensnare alas,

Do I dare-
Heed such desires which may,
Rouse the beast from its long forgotten
lair,

Hold, hold chain about my neck!
Verily, thou art a man civilized,
Elevated from the base,
Hold! I charge thee lest
I am given to gorge myself on human
flesh!

Bore not of malady,
Nor sin,
For one and all,
There lies in wait,
The animal within.

This lone act of vile import,
In the prodigious machinations of this
world,
Is venial, yes?

There are others, surely,
Who even now,
Art engaged in doings of a worser
sort?

Lo, mine hunger is not so easily
appeased,
With ferocity, I did lunge,
Towards that limb where it lay,
As by another fraction that chain gave
way.

To devour my late companion to
sustain my labours-
Far better I perish,
I cannot forfeit my humanity,
On account of a fatal deed so garish!

Thus resolved,
I wrapped my offending limbs more
soundly in their manacles,
Whilst imploring the mortar to grip that
chain without fail,
In a last bid to tame the animal!

Peradventure,
These means werst afforded to stave
my plaguing hunger,
If I take not this meat, doubtless wilt
another.

That chain burst to the final link,
As I fell upon that corse with unbridled
savagery,
Know thee not,
That no chain is proof against primeval
instinct!

Know thee not that amongst all men,
Art those who time and time again,
Wilt to their bloodlust yield,
Mastered wholly by the beast of the
field?

By tooth and nail in the transports of
frenzy,
I tore the meat from the bone,
In a horrid display that was not to
cease,
Until I was clad in the gore that belies
the beast.

Body crouched-
cruel and viscous,
Teeth bare for some deadly purpose ,
Eyes darting with a luster fell, a luster
keen.

To man,
There remained no semblance,
To be seen.

How long might I endure?
Thought I, spent from the carnage,
Sprawled there upon the floor.

How long will his remains give satiety?

For therein that dungeon's recesses,
Were scores of rats with their own
hunger to be quelled,
Scores of rats,
With their own designs for me.

So was the end to my plight,
Here in my tomb consigned,
Dark as a murder of crows,
On a winters midnight.

This is where it all....

ENDS